Aimless Analects

Aliyah Saddler

BookLeaf
Publishing

India | USA | UK

Presentation by *BookLeaf Publishing*

Web: www.bookleafpub.com

E-mail: info@bookleafpub.com

ISBN: 9789357446006

First edition 2022

DEDICATION

I'd like to dedicate this to YHWH. I prayed a specific prayer and You answered.

Also to my mom, of course!

Lemonade

Life presented lemons,
it was up to me to unearth the other ingredients.
Lemonade isn't made just by squeezing a lemon.
I had to search my soul for what I was missing.
Water came from the Well that never runs dry.
Everlasting spiritual hydration.
Combining lemons with water lacks flavor.
I needed an element of sweetness.
Passion.
Passion was my sugar.
My lemonade tastes like perseverance.
Have a sip.

4:06 am

Awake.
So many thoughts want to flood my mind, but I
use social media as a dam.
I scroll for miles, every post and video another
stick to add to the dam's "protection."
But the dam leaks.
(I've never been great at assembling. Perhaps
that explains my brokenness).
Occasionally, a thought slips from the security
of my twigged wall.
Rushing behind one thought is the sea of
thoughts so desperately wanting to be addressed.
Most of them derive from anxiety…
an anxiety that I try to keep at bay.
Nobody else takes it serious, why should I?
Even now, anxious thoughts attempt to crowd
my mind.
I wish I wasn't so afraid of myself.
Essentially that's what it boils down to.
I compare myself to everyone, hoping that I'm
good enough.
Why isn't it enough that I'm good?

Empty Embrace

You don't hug me with two arms, anymore.
Just one of your members reaches around my
neck and holds tight.
It's supposed to be an embrace, it feels like
suffocation.
The irony. I can't breathe when you're not
squeezing me.
Why don't you hug me fully, anymore?
Do you find me undeserving of your
completeness?
Though your other arm stays low, I imagine it is
a shield.
Do you not trust me anymore?
We used to stand in the middle of rooms and
hold each other for many seconds.
Mini seconds, now do our hugs last.
Every single one shorter than the last.
Why don't you hug me with two arms, anymore?

Suspect of Narcissism

My least favorite thing is when somebody plays victim after being the suspect.
When someone murders their entire family, and then cries about the cold blood they get in return.
How narcissistic of you to expect warmth from people you constantly abuse.
You're ashamed of us.
You think you're better than us.
But when we accept that you want nothing to do with us, you cry that no one loves you.
You want love from people you claim you hate.
Or are you liar?
Maybe you do love us?
Maybe you do love us but we don't fit into the life you imagined?
It's hard to care.

Choose Peace

We preach peace,
but only the kind that involves us.
We say, "choose peace,"
with an invisible subtitle that says, "choose me."
Peace doesn't always include you.
In fact, peace is sometimes the very opposite of
you.
Sometimes you are every violent, crashing wave
to a ship trying desperately to get to its
destination.
Hard pill to swallow, but you have to.

Love Language

You want me to speak your love language.
A language not only foreign to me,
but unbearably uncomfortable for me to speak.
But I learned it.
Not speaking it as often as you wanted me to
made you feel rejected.
So I hugged you and accepted hugs from you,
even when it made my body tighten and my skin
crawl.
But you don't care that speaking your language
makes me sick.
You just love that I speak it through the sickness.
Not to mention that my language is ignored
unless I speak yours.
You've used something that was supposed to be
beautiful and helpful,
and turned it into a weapon of manipulation.
You don't speak love.
You emotionally abuse people into giving you
what you want.
That's not love.

Coffee

I awaken to the aroma of your beautiful
blackness
I sigh with bliss.
I can't wait to taste you.
I'm afraid if I don't have you soon I'll lose
energy.
I am grumpy when you're not in my hands.
Many people will experience you differently,
today.
I want you in your simplest state.
Black and strong.
You've been brewing a while.
I'll drink you now.
Coffee, my love.

Hold You

I want to hold you.
Feel the warmth of your existence.
Our bodies seem to fit perfectly together,
like you were shaped for me.
I want to carry you.
It goes so far beyond your body.
Tell me everything that's wrong.
I want to fix it all.
I want to cuddle you.
Protect you from the world.
Protect you from your world.
Protect you.
But I'm not supposed to.
I used to hold you.
I used to carry you.
I used to cuddle you.
But I was never supposed to.

I Caught the Bouquet

I caught the bouquet!
When does my forever begin?
Oh to love a man who is only mine.
And to be loved so deeply it surpasses time.
Oh to have a family of my own.
To look at my child and see a clone.
Dear God, You know I crave love so deep.
Perhaps there is something wrong with me?
There has to be.
Why else would I not have my wildest dream?
Hopeless romantic, still with an ounce of hope.
Because I caught the bouquet...
Where's my happily ever after?

Too Good

He must be a fallen speck of the sun.
When he smiles the planets align.
My world is a little bit brighter.
He is far away, but I feel his warmth.
Even when I'm hiding under clouds
I am still blessed by his existence.
I'm sure he doesn't intend to,
but he makes me smile.
He's a breath of fresh air.
He's not just the breath,
he's the fresh air.
I breathe him in slowly.
The air hasn't been this fresh in a while.
He's become a good friend.
My very own comedian.
And he speaks his mind.
He encourages me to speak mine.
He's not afraid of me.
I am afraid of him.

6/25/2020

I've not been present lately.
Living in my mind and not the moment.
I'm losing myself.
A mere shadow of who I used to be.
I don't who this person is.
I look in the mirror and can hardly recognize this
person.
This person isn't full of vibrancy.
She seems void of any good feeling.
I am not just sad. No.
There's something much deeper than sadness
trying to express itself.
I feel too much.
Every emotion comes in like waves.
Soft at first, but then strong enough to take me
out.
I am tired.
Tired in ways that sleep won't aid.

Still In Love

Allow me to be the first to admit,
I'm still in love with you.
I know, I'm not supposed love you this way.
My heart has always been defiant.
You are forbidden fruit.
I am only allowed to admire you from afar.
The slightest nibble would kill me.
When I don't have fight in me,
death for you sounds like a fantasy.
But when sense is knocked into me,
I know it's best to eat.
What I'm allowed to eat is in greater quantity.
And the quality is much better, too.

The End

Maybe the earth was soulless.
It didn't have vibrancy anymore.
It didn't rain much, either.
Maybe she had no tears left to cry.
The earth was a mere shadow of what she used
to be.
Trees didn't grow leaves anymore.
There was no need for photosynthesis with no
sun.
Instead, tall trunks cried out for mercy with their
hundreds of outstretched arms.
It was hard to notice at first, but grass didn't
exist anymore.
Where grass used to be, vast acres of hard dirt
covered it.
Colors were a memory.
The bright yellows, vivacious pinks,
sophisticated purples, vibrant reds; everything
was gray.
Earth tones weren't green, brown, or burnt
orange, anymore.
Earth only had one tone, now: dead.

Organ

In science they teach you that the heart is the
most vital organ...
maybe that's why you keep playing mine.
Do you enjoy the sounds of my tears hitting the
pillowcase?
Or maybe you just enjoy knowing
that of all the people who've gotten ahold of it...
you play it best.

A Jazz Song

A saxophone starts the ballad.
It's dark before she cries her golden notes into
the room.
She's crying about the tragedy of love.
Melodious high notes that decrescendo into
bitter low ones.
While she cries, a piano accompanies her.
Careful not to speak over the saxophone,
the piano gently offers her condolences.
She is gentle the whole time,
only speaking up during the breaks of the sax.
A snare and hi-hat ease their way into the pity.
They simply guide the girls through the pain.
The snare and hi-hat barely whisper.
They speak loud enough to let them know
they're there.
The room is a bit brighter now, though the mood
is still dark.
Saxophone continues to wail,
piano gets a little louder in her sorrow,
snare and hi-hat continue to whisper.
Piano embraces the saxophone,
snare and hi-hat hush,
and saxophone lets out one last cry.
The ballad ends.

Novel

He was a book I so desperately wanted to read,
but every other page was glued together.
I wanted to open him up,
but I knew that I needed to be careful
or else I'd do more harm than good.
Instead of ripping him apart,
I read what was presented.
Choppy, yes.
But still I was interested.
Even with pieces of him hidden from me,
he was the most amazing story I'd ever read.
He became my favorite book.
Yes, I praised the Author of his story for writing
him so well.
But even good stories get old.
Just as the thought came to close him for good,
and put him away on a shelf for someone else to
read,
he began to unseal the pages once hidden.

Woman

Created by God,
From man,
For man,
I am a woman.
I am man inside out.
I said I am man's insides out.
I am a woman.
A wombed man.
A man with a womb.
I am a woman.
Not taken from his cranium,
cause then I'd be above him.
Not taken from his spine,
cause then I'd be behind him.
Not taken from his heel,
cause then I'd be under him.
I am a woman.
Taken from his rib.
To be by his side.
I am a woman.
Created to intake.
Created to create.
Created to create with what I intake
And to intake what I create.
I am a woman

Better

You said you left to better yourself.
Crazy that I wasn't apart of your better.
I understand that I was only part of your world.
Why can't you understand that you were my
whole world?
You were the first man I've ever loved.
You were supposed to be there for me.
Why weren't you there for me?
Oh, right.
Better.
You had to go find better because I wasn't
enough.
Why wasn't I enough?
It's because of you that I feel inadequate.
If my first love could walk away that easily,
why would anyone else stay?
I'm not good enough.
Did you find the better you were looking for?
Of course you did because you left me.
Why did you leave me?

No More

Maybe I feel ugly because I am ugly.
There's only a matter of time before what's
inside of me comes out.
The sin I've been trying to hide is oozing from
me.
What I see when I look at the in the mirror isn't
beautiful because I've defiled myself.
King's kid wallowing in the pigsty.
I can't continue like this.
I have to be free, even if that means biting the
chains off, one by one.
I can't keep going in this manner.
Souls are drowning, and there's a possibility that
my sin is keeping their head underwater.
No more.
No. More.
Too many lives depend on my obedience.

Choose Me

From the day that I formed you,
I knew I'd choose you no matter what.
In every lifetime,
in any universe,
I'd choose you.
You haven't made that easy,
but I vowed that no matter your attitude,
no matter your decisions,
I'd always choose you.
What do I want in return?
I just want you to choose Me for once.
Not out of convenience.
Choose Me because you love Me.
Choose Me because I love you.
Choose Me because I gave My life choosing
you,
and I'd do it again.

Here She Comes

The more I stare into the mirror of my soul,
the more I see myself for who I am.
I'm afraid of who I see.
She's much greater than who I've accepted
myself to be.
She is joy personified, love unquantified.
She has no limits.
She just is.
She breathes deep and releases the air slow.
Out of her heart does the love of her Father flow.
She is everything I've ever dreamed of being.
Then I stare at the eyes in my reflection.
They tell me the story of her arrival.
My eyes widen.
She should be here soon...

www.ingramcontent.com/pod-product-compliance
Lightning Source LLC
LaVergne TN
LVHW050258200726
843509LV00015B/3067